The Book of Kindness

慈

The Book of Kindness
Power of the Gentle Path

Compiled by
Mary Lou Cook
Jan Lurie
Richard Polese

OCEAN TREE BOOKS
Santa Fe, New Mexico

The compilers are grateful to the many contributors to this book, past and living. We have made our best effort to respect everybody's creative rights. It has been difficult to find the original sources of some anecdotal material. We offer our sincere apology for any unintentional infringement or incorrect or improper attribution.

(The Chinese characters represent aspects of human kindness.)

First Edition. Printed in North America.

OCEAN TREE BOOKS

Post Office Box 1295
Santa Fe, New Mexico 87504
(505) 983-1412
www.oceantree.com

Design/Production: SunFlower Designs of Santa Fe
Cover Design: Caren Cook

Published in

ISBN: 978-0-943734-47-7

Library of Congress CIP Data:

The book of kindness : power of the gentle path / compiled by
Mary Lou Cook, Jan Lurie, Richard Polese. — 1st ed.
     p.   cm.
Includes bibliographical references.
ISBN 978-0-943734-47-7 (alk. paper)
1. Kindness.   2. Kindness—Quotations, maxims, etc.
    I. Cook, Mary Lou. 1918–   II. Lurie, Jan. 1930–
III. Polese, Richard. 1941–
BJ1533.K5B66 2007
177'.7—dc22
2007037753

Dedicated to the
Spirit of Kindness in Everyone

We wish especially to recognize examples of kindness that came from the hearts of these people, both ordinary and well-known: Catherine Ryan Hyde and the Pay It Forward Foundation, His Holiness the Fourteenth Dalai Lama, President Jimmy Carter, Mata Amritanandama (Ammachi), Martin Luther King Jr., Mike McGurl, Muhammad Yunus and the Grameen Bank, Mohandas Gandhi, Nelson Mandela, Mother Theresa, Nicole Paultre, Peace Pilgrim, Princess Diana, Ryan (of *Ryan's Well),* Raoul Wallenberg, Samantha Smith, Therese of Liseaux, Wangari Maathai, the Agua Fria Elementary School students of teachers Christina Pavlak and Lisa Randall, the church people rebuilding homes in New Orleans, the many volunteers of the United States Peace Corps and Habitat for Humanity, and grandparents everywhere.

Contents

An Introduction

Some things are simple, yet powerful. For many of us in this country and culture, the world seems vastly complicated and difficult and becoming more so—all the way from family relations to the establishment of a peaceful and sustainable world.

It dawned on the three of us that in most of these circumstances one thing is continually overlooked or given short shrift, perhaps because it seems almost too quiet: simple human kindness.

We have come to realize that simple kindness to others, to oneself, and all that lives and breathes, is possibly the most transformative force of all. We have come to see that the greatest need of today's humanity is the understanding and use of genuine, heartfelt communication, and that the failure to care for others is at the root of most human problems. Will our world survive? Very likely it will, when we learn to regard each other with a few more ounces of kindness.

Humankind has seen and made for itself many advances—in communications, transportation, technology, health, science, convenience—these are a wonder! Yet collectively (and perhaps individually) we lag in the areas of the heart, soul, spirit: how to get along with one another and even with the deepest parts of ourselves. What would result if more and more of us began to shift our attention to feelings and expressions of gratitude, the pleasure of sharing, having and offering hope, forgiveness, being happy, honoring our intuitive potential, having fun, accepting blessings, and nurturing inner peace and inner strength?

We join with the millions who weep with the misery of the many who suffer from the wars and personal violence going on all over the world. Senseless deaths, bodies and brains maimed, families broken, homeless and hungry refugees, and billions in resources being spent on armaments and the craft of killing, with insane plans for ever more clever and effective weapons of human destruction.

We all ask what can a single person do to help change all this? What could lift us from the thousands of hurts and hates and loneliness of life today? Most everyone wants peace on our earth, but where do we start? Isn't it time to pause and see if we have overlooked something basic?

Let's start here, with these simple yet profound reminders of what it means to be kind. In this book you will find the words of wise leaders and teachers, philosophers, and plain folks, all on the subject of Kindness. Our job is loving, learning, helping, being happy, and giving others a hand along their paths.

With quiet joy, we have compiled this little book of quotes, actions, inspiration, and ideas. We hope that its value and support may start a movement of kindness, replacing the impulse to continuing violence of every form.

Imagine a culture of kindness: with mostly happy and positive people, with only a hazy memory of wars, and with disputes settled through patience, diplomacy, and seeing another's point of view. With civility practiced in family life, business and politics. With a revolutionary movement to enact peace and justice. With media focused on positive and helpful stories. With a national department of peacemaking to overcome misunderstanding, greed, and the misuse of power. Imagine these words translated into many other languages. Imagine people wearing kindness as a universally understood and appreciated virtue (see page 42). This is the world as most of us wish it to become.

We do not have to settle for the way things have always been done, which really has not worked too well. We three have discovered that big, complicated plans and grueling effort often exhaust one or make one anxious and angry. And yet, if we want change, we all must do something differently.

Why not try something so simple, so basic, often elusive, but ultimately so powerful as the impulse to kindness? It takes little learning and the practice of it is so fruitful.

Kindness is something we can offer to everyone every day — in small ways, in big ways, in easy ways, sometimes in ways that take an extra ounce of courage. We can adopt it as an attitude to all life. We can let it begin to heal our relationships. We can let it open our hearts and minds to people near at home and far away in other lands.

We are finding that the regular practice of kindness is indeed powerful — like gravity or sunlight, its effects recur and endure — changing moments, sometimes changing lives, perhaps changing the world.

The world is a beautiful place. As we begin to practice kindness more and more, the beauty of the world and the life we all share become more and more evident.

Peace be with you.

Kindness be with you!

Mary Lou Cook
Jan Lurie
Richard Polese

仁慈仁慈仁慈仁慈仁慈仁慈

If you want to be understood, practice kindness and mercy. Kindness is seldom mistaken for anything else. Small kindnesses reverberate a long time in people's hearts.

A woman checking IDs at the airport saw me coming the other day and said, "Good morning, Sunshine." She didn't know me from Adam. She glanced at my driver's license and said "Have a good flight, darling." This was in the South, of course — in Austin, Texas to be exact. Northern women would no sooner address a strange man as Sunshine than they would ask if you wanted to see their underwear. But that woman's Sunshine shone on me for the rest of the day, and a week later I still remember it. Like I remember old waitresses in diners who addressed everyone as Love. "Care for more coffee, Love?" Yes, dear. And you left a quarter tip instead of a dime. Fifteen cents for a little endearment.

— *Garrison Keillor*

仁慈仁慈仁慈仁慈仁慈仁慈

慈

1

The Nature of Kindness

Kindness is an inner desire that makes us want to do good things even if we do not get anything in return. It is the joy of our life to do them. When we do good things from this inner desire, there is kindness in everything we think, say and do.

Emanuel Swedenborg

Love is patient, love is kind. It is not jealous, it is not pompous, it is not proud. It is not rude, it is not self-seeking, it is not easily angered, it keeps no record of wrong.

Paul's First Letter to the Corinthians 13:4

Kindness is in our power, even when fondness is not.

Samuel Johnson

A kind word is like a spring day.

Russian proverb

Kindness is a language which the dumb can speak, the deaf can understand.

C. N. Bovee

This only is charity: to do all, all that we can.

John Donne

The hearts of those we touch are opened, and they in turn touch the hearts of others... This expression of our deepest nature is the living power of loving kindness — as the Buddha said, "it glows, it shines, it blazes forth."

Tara Brach

Goodness is uneventful. It does not flash, it glows.

David Grayson

Kindness is an energy – a loving and sympathetic flow of energy that comes from deep in the heart of humanity. It is strong and supportive and the action springs from the energy flow... We cannot judge others and then proclaim kindness. The energy flow of kindness goes out with no strings attached.

Paula J. Hunter and Shri Kingsford

What wisdom can you find that is greater than kindness?

Jean Jacques Rousseau

The highest form of wisdom is kindness.

The Talmud

The end result of wisdom is...good deeds.

The Babylonian Talmud

Kindness is more than deeds. It is an attitude, an expression, a look, a touch. It is anything that lifts another person.

Ralph Scott

仁慈仁慈仁慈仁慈仁慈仁慈

During my second year of nursing school our professor gave us a quiz. I breezed through the questions until I read the last one: What was the first name of the woman who cleans the school?

Surely this was a joke. I had seen the woman several times, but how would I know her name? I handed in my paper, leaving the question blank. Before the class ended, one student asked if the last question would count toward our grade. "Absolutely," the professor said. "In your careers you will meet many people. All are significant. They deserve your attention and care, even if all you do is smile and say hello."

I've never forgotten that lesson. I also learned her name was Dorothy.

—*Joann C. James*

仁慈仁慈仁慈仁慈仁慈仁慈

A warm smile is the universal language of kindness.

William Arthur Ward

Kindness is tolerance (the absence of judgment)
Kindness is gentleness (the absence of harm)
Kindness is generosity (the absence of selfishness)

Kenneth Wapnick

...How does it feel when someone stops to let you in, and maybe even smiles? That is what kindness feels like.

Piero Ferrucci

Kindness is the ability to love someone more than they deserve.

Anonymous

Kindness in ourselves is the honey that blunts the sting of unkindness in others.

Walter Lander

We cannot be just unless we are kind.

Luc de Clapiers Vauvenargues

Loving kindness is greater than laws.

The Talmud

Kindness is love, but perhaps greater than love.
Kindness says, I want you to be happy.

Randolph Ray

True kindness presupposes the faculty of
imagining as one's own the sufferings and
joys of others.

Andre Gide

Remember there's no such thing as a small act
of kindness. Every act creates a ripple with no
logical ends.

Scott Adams

Kindness gives birth to kindness.

Sophocles

No act of kindness, no matter how small,
is ever wasted.

Aesop

Thoughtfulness, the kindly regard for others,
is the beginning of holiness.

Mother Theresa

Real generosity is doing something nice for
someone who will never find out.

Frank A. Clark

Kindness is gladdening the hearts of those
who are traveling with us.

Henri F. Amiel

Where kindness leads happiness follows.

Meg Schutte

[For soldiers in combat] The only solace comes
from simple acts of kindness. They are the
flickering candles in a cavern of darkness
that sustain our common humanity.

Chris Hedges

Kindness is the evidence of greatness. If anyone is glad you are here, then you have not lived in vain.

Charles Fenno Hoffman

Kind words are the music of the world. They have a power which seems to be beyond natural causes, as if they were some angel's song which had lost its way and come to earth.

Frederich W. Faber

Kindness, I've discovered, is everything in life.

Isaac Bashevis Singer

慈

2

Importance of Kindness to Civilization

Civilization is just a slow process of learning to be kind.

Charles L. Lucas

...the real law lives in the kindness of our hearts. If our hearts are empty, no law or political reform can fill them.

Leo Tolstoy

The word kindness comes from kin, meaning all one family.

Anonymous

He who is kind and courteous to strangers thereby shows himself a citizen of the world.

Anonymous

Kindness is the golden chain by which society is bound together.

Johann Wolfgang Von Goethe

Until he extends the circle of his compassion to all living things, man will not himself find peace.

Albert Schweitzer

The key to joy is the unconditional kindness to all life, including one's own, that we refer to as compassion. Without compassion little of any significance is ever accomplished in human endeavor.

David R. Hawkins

Compassion is the chief law of human existence.

Fyodor Dostoyevsky

It is good and right to be happy. It is also the only way I can be consistently kind to myself.

Hugh Prather

All of us owe our very existence to the kindness of those who came before us, even if it was only the act of being fed when we were a helpless infant.

Jan Lurie

Almost anything you do will seem insignificant, but it is very important that you do it.

Mohandas Gandhi

Service is the rent we pay for being. It is the very purpose of life and not something you do in your spare time.

Marian Wright Edelman

Politicians have issues. Be kind to them. Then you are being kind to yourself.

Gary Renard

Kindness is the bridge to life's opportunities.

found on the seal of a carton of Daisy Sour Cream

Kindness expiates a multitude of sins.

Anonymous

Deeds of kindness are equal in weight to all the commandments.

The Talmud

Whoever is kind to his creatures, God is kind to him.

Mohammed

A person's true wealth is the good he or she does in the world.

Mohammed

Three things in life are important. The first is to be kind. The second is to be kind. The third is to be kind.

Henry James

When you are kind to someone in trouble, you hope they'll remember and be kind to someone else. And it'll become like a wildfire.

Whoopie Goldberg

It's a bit embarrassing to have been concerned with the human problem all one's life and find out at the end that one has no more to offer by way of advice than "try to be a little kinder."

Aldous Huxley

Compassion is the desire that moves the individual self to widen the scope of its self-concern to embrace the whole of the universal self.

Arnold Toynbee

If we make our goal to live a life of compassion and unconditional love, then the world will indeed become a garden where all kinds of flowers can bloom and grow.

Elisabeth Kubler-Ross

If the instinctual and repressed kindness of mankind were suddenly let loose upon the earth, sooner than we think we would be members one of another, sitting around one family hearthstone and singing the song of new humanity.

George D. Herron

慈

3

The Practice of Kindness

Be kind, for everyone you meet is fighting a hard battle.

Plato

When you carry out acts of kindness you get a wonderful feeling inside. It is as though something inside your body responds and says, Yes, this is how I ought to feel.

Harold S. Kushner

If you judge people you have no time to love them.

Chinese proverb

Be kind to unkind people; they need it the most.

Chinese proverb

Always meet petulance and perverseness with gentleness. A gentle hand can lead even an elephant by a hair.

Zoroaster

The love of your neighbor in all its fullness simply means being able to say to him, "What are you going through?"

Simone Weil

If you want others to be happy, practice compassion. If you want to be happy, practice compassion.

The Fourteenth Dalai Lama

Compassion is not looked upon as a virtue. Nevertheless, the...sages discovered by trial and error that if you did behave in a consistently compassionate way, you encountered a greater reach of the divine within yourself. But you had to do it. It's a method, not just a belief system. It's a method that has to be put into practice.

Karen Armstrong

When we remember over and over how much we long to be tender and kind, and let ourselves fully inhabit that longing, compassion naturally awakens.

Tara Brach

Let no one come to you without leaving better and happier. Be the living expression of God's kindness: kindness in your face, kindness in your eyes, kindness in your smile.

Mother Theresa

Keep doing good deeds long enough, and you'll probably turn out a good man in spite of yourself.

Louis Auchincloss

Where there is a human being, there is an opportunity for kindness.

Seneca

仁慈仁慈仁慈仁慈仁慈仁慈

In the days when an ice cream sundae cost much less, a 10-year-old boy entered a hotel coffee shop and sat at a table. A waitress put a glass of water in front of him. "How much is an ice cream sundae?" he asked. "Fifty cents," replied the waitress. The little boy pulled his hand out of his pocket and studied the coins in it.

"Well, how much is a plain dish of ice cream?" he inquired.

By now more people were waiting for a table and the waitress was growing impatient. "Thirty-five cents," she brusquely replied. The little boy counted his coins. "I'll have the plain ice cream," he said.

The waitress brought the ice cream, put the bill on the table and walked away. The boy finished the ice cream, paid the cashier and left. When the waitress came back, she began to cry as she wiped down the table. There placed neatly beside the empty dish, were two nickels and five pennies.

You see, he couldn't have the sundae, because he had to have enough left to leave her a tip.

仁慈仁慈仁慈仁慈仁慈仁慈

One can always be kind to people about whom one cares nothing.

Oscar Wilde

There isn't anyone who can't be treated kindly, because how I treat others is up to me.

Hugh Prather

Let me be a little kinder, let me be a little blinder to the faults of those around me.

Edgar A. Guest

If you can't be kind, at least have the decency to be vague.

Anonymous

If your words are soft and sweet, they won't be as hard to swallow if you have to eat them.

Anonymous

仁慈仁慈仁慈仁慈仁慈仁慈

A Jew going on a trip from Jerusalem to Jericho was
attacked by bandits. They stripped him of his clothes and
money and beat him up and left him lying half dead
beside the road. By chance a Jewish priest came along;
and when he saw the man lying there, he crossed to the
other side of the road and passed him by. A Jewish
temple assistant walked over and looked at him lying
there, but then went on.

But a despised Samaritan came along and when he
saw him he felt deep pity. Kneeling beside him the
Samaritan soothed his wounds with medicine and band-
aged them. Then he put the man on his donkey and
walked along beside him till they came to an inn, where
he nursed him through the night.

The next day he handed the innkeeper two denarii and
told him to take care of the man. "If his bill runs higher
than that," he said, "I'll pay the difference the next time I
am here."

— Jesus, in Luke 10:30-35

We are called to play the good Samaritan on life's
roadside: but that will be only an initial act. One day the
whole Jericho road must be transformed so that men and
women will not be beaten and robbed as they make their
journey through life. True compassion is more than fling-
ing a coin to a beggar.

— Martin Luther King, Jr.

仁慈仁慈仁慈仁慈仁慈仁慈

Never miss an opportunity to make others happy, even if you have to leave them alone in order to do it.

Anonymous

You can never do a kindness too soon, because you never know how soon it will be too late.

Ralph Waldo Emerson

And be kind to one another, tenderhearted, forgiving one another, even as God has forgiven you.

Paul's Letter to the Ephesians 4:32

What you do not want done to yourself do not do to others.

Confucius

Do for others what you would have them to do for you. For this sums up the Law and the Prophets.

Jesus' Sermon on the Mount, Matthew 7:12

We have committed the Golden Rule to memory; let us now commit it to life.

Edwin Markham

You have not lived a perfect day, even though you have earned your money, unless you have done something for someone who cannot repay you.

Ruth Smeltzer

If you stop to be kind, you must swerve often from your path...

Mary Webb

After the verb "to love," the verb "to help" is the most beautiful verb in the world.

Bertha Von Suttner

If ever we can be free of the need to get there first, do more, earn more, then other people will no longer appear as obstacles to our urgency. We will feel kinder toward them.

Piero Ferrucci

I expect to pass through the world but once; any good thing therefore that I can do, or any kindness that I can show to any fellow creature, let me do it now; let me not defer or neglect it, for I shall not pass this way again.

attributed to Stephen Grellet, William Penn, others

It is the characteristic of the magnanimous man to ask no favor but to be ready to do kindness to others.

Aristotle

To practice five things everywhere under heaven constitutes perfect virtue...gravity, generosity of soul, sincerity, earnestness, and kindness.

Confucius

仁慈仁慈仁慈仁慈仁慈仁慈

As the bus slowed down at the crowded bus stop, the Pakistani bus conductor leaned from the platform and called out, "Six only!" The bus stopped. He counted on six passengers, rang the bell, then as the bus moved off, called to those left behind, "So sorry, plenty of room in my heart, but the bus is full." He left behind a row of smiling faces.

It is not what you do, it's the way you do it.

— *Anonymous*

仁慈仁慈仁慈仁慈仁慈仁慈

There are times that when truth and kindness conflict one ought to choose kindness, especially when a little honesty is better than a lot.

Leroy Jack Syrop

Great opportunities to help others seldom come, but small ones surround us daily.

Sally Koch

Don't wait for people to be friendly, show them how.

Anonymous

Waste no more time arguing what a good man should be. Be one!

Marcus Aurelius

慈

4

Kindness Is Not Weakness

*Kindness has taken a bad rap in many ways,
being associated with weakness or meekness or
labels like "goody-goody." But true kindness
comes from strength, and is full of life.*

Bo Lozoff

*The greatness of man can nearly always be
measured by his willingness to be kind.*

Michel Simon

They're only truly great who are truly good.

George Chapman

*The weak can never forgive. Forgiveness is the
attribute of the strong.*

Mohandas Gandhi

It is the weak who are cruel. Gentleness can only be expected from the strong...

Leo Rosten

Can I see another's woe, and not be in sorrow too? Can I see another's grief, and not seek for kind relief?

William Blake

When kindness has left people, even for a few moments, we become afraid of them, as if their reason has left them...

Willa Cather

Human kindness has never weakened the stamina or softened the fiber of a free people. A nation does not have to be cruel in order to be tough.

Franklin D. Roosevelt

Gentleness is not a quality exclusive to women.

Helen Reddy

Each person has inside a basic decency and goodness. If he listens to it and acts on it, he is giving a great deal of what it is the world needs most. It is not complicated but it takes courage. It takes courage for a person to listen to his own goodness and act on it.

Pablo Casals

Women like men who are kind.
Men like women who are kind.
Who wants to spend time with people who aren't?

Mary Lou Cook and Jan Lurie

I think women need kindness more than love.

Alice Childress

A woman would have run through fire and water for such a kind heart.

William Shakespeare

Just because an animal is large, it doesn't mean he doesn't want kindness; however big Tigger seems to be, remember that he wants as much kindness as Roo.

A. A. Milne

仁慈仁慈仁慈仁慈仁慈仁慈

Many years ago, a little girl named Liz was suffering from a rare and serious disease. Her only chance of recovery appeared to be a blood transfusion from her five-year-old brother, who had miraculously survived the same disease and had developed the antibodies needed to combat the illness. The doctor explained the situation to her little brother, and asked the little boy if he would be willing to give his blood to his sister.

He hesitated for only a moment before taking a deep breath and saying, "Yes, I'll do it if it will save her." As the transfusion progressed, he lay in bed next to his sister and smiled, as we all did, seeing the color returning to her cheeks. Then his face grew pale and his smile faded.

He looked up at the doctor and asked with a trembling voice, "Will I start to die right away?"

Being young, the little boy had misunderstood the doctor; he thought he was going to have to give his sister all of his blood in order to save her.

仁慈仁慈仁慈仁慈仁慈仁慈

慈

5

Kindness as a Way of Being in the World

Kindness is the root of righteousness.
Kindness is the enemy of cruelty, harshness,
rudeness. It softens the heart. It opens the
door to heaven...

Sivananda

No one appears inferior to us when our
heart is kindled with kindness.

Hazrat Inayat Khan

Kindness is the opposite of judgment.

A Course in Miracles

*This is my simple religion. There is no need
for complicated philosophy. Our own brain,
our own heart is our temple; the philosophy is
kindness.*

The Fourteenth Dalai Lama

*One who knows how to show and accept
kindness will be a friend better than any
possession.*

Sophocles

*The everyday kindness of the roads more than
makes up for the greed in the headlines.*

Charles Kuralt

*...whenever you reach out in loving kindness,
you are expressing God.*

Peace Pilgrim

It is when you give of yourself that you
truly give.

Kahlil Gibran

I do not give lectures or a little charity. When
I give, I give myself.

Walt Whitman

...just being ordinary in itself is an expression
of divinity...to live with care and kindness is
all that is necessary.

David R. Hawkins

It is easy enough to be friendly to one's friends.
But to befriend the one who regards himself as
your enemy is the quintessence of true religion.
The other is mere business.

Mohandas Gandhi

If we are kind we'll have joy.

Betty Eadie

What you do for yourself — any gesture of kindness, any gesture of gentleness, any gesture of honesty and clear seeing toward yourself — will affect how you experience your world. In fact it will transform how you experience the world.

Pema Chödrön

*If I can stop one heart from breaking,
I shall not live in vain:
If I can ease one life the aching,
Or cool one pain,
Or help one fainting robin unto his nest again,
I shall not live in vain.*

Emily Dickinson

Kindness can become its own motive. We are made kind by being kind.

Eric Hoffer

Goodness is achieved not in a vacuum, but in the company of other men, attended by love.

Saul Bellow

...in learning how to be kind to another person, you are practicing being kind to yourself...

Kenneth Wapnick

It is one of the most beautiful compensations of life that no man can sincerely try to help another without helping himself.

Ralph Waldo Emerson

*Kindness requires us to become more awake
and aware —
aware of the feelings and needs of others
aware of our own fears and defenses.
The more we practice kindness the more
conscious we become.
We become who we were meant to be.*

Jan Lurie

*Kindness in words creates confidence.
Kindness in thinking creates profoundness.
Kindness in giving creates love.*

Lao Tzu

*The simple gift of being kind is greater than
all the wisdom of the wise.*

DuBose Heyward

Men are only great as they are kind.

Elbert Hubbard

We make a living by what we get, but we make a life by what we give.

Norman MacEswan

What you give is a life; what you get is a living.

Lillian Gish

There is no choice between being kind to others and being kind to ourselves. It is the same thing.

Piero Ferrucci

The older you get, the more you realize that kindness is synonymous with happiness.

Lionel Barrymore

That best portion of a good man's life
His little nameless unremembered acts
Of kindness and of love.

William Wordsworth

When I was young, I used to admire intelligent people; as I got older, I admire kind people.

Abraham Joshua Heschel

A human being is a part of the whole that we call the universe, a part limited in time and space. He experiences himself, his thoughts and feelings, as something separated from the rest — a kind of optical illusion of his consciousness. This illusion is a prison for us, restricting us to our personal desires and to affection for only the few people nearest us. Our task must be to free ourselves from this prison by widening our circle of compassion to embrace all living beings and all of nature.

Albert Einstein

Beginning today treat everyone you meet as if they were going to be dead by midnight. Extend to them all the care, kindness and understanding you can muster, and do it with no thought of any reward. Your life will never be the same again.

Og Mandino

The world is too big, too stubborn in its ways for any combination of us to "save" it. All we are called to do is to act kindly, responsibly and attentively within the limits our lives impose on us. If enough of us do that, the healing will begin.

Scott Russell Sanders

慈

Verbs of Kindness

Kindness disarms.

Kindness helps to find the common ground.

Kindness heals wounds.

Kindness lightens life's burdens.

Kindness breaks though resistance.

Kindness tames the savage.

Kindness overcomes anger.

Kindness discovers love that lies dormant.

Kindness rekindles friendship.

Kindness reconciles...

Kindness overcomes...

Kindness breaks through...

Kindness draws the impulse to peace.

— Richard Polese

The World Kindness Bracelet

This simple bracelet will serve to remind you to keep *Kindness* as a guiding norm of your life—the way you choose to relate to yourself, those you encounter, and the whole world.

On the MLC World Bracelet, the word "Kindness" is inscribed in 17 languages,* gently affirming that kindness is a universal and powerfully transformative virtue. Made of soft silicon material that's easy to wear, this bracelet serves to nurture your commitment to the healing of all life on the planet—through daily expressions of kindness towards yourself and all that lives.

We suggest that the wearer look at his or her World Bracelet every day at noon, joining the millions of others who have made a similar commitment to kindness.

The World Kindness Bracelet is a gift. If you wish to join us in spreading this symbol of active kindness, you may make a donation to the Mary Lou Cook Creativity Center. Let us know how many you'd like us to send to you to share with friends. This will help keep the project going, and spread ripples of kindness around the world!

Mary Lou Cook Creativity Center
PO Box 24271, Santa Fe, New Mexico 87502 USA

(505) 983-5410 • *www.worldbracelet.org*

*English, Korean, Vietnamese, Portuguese, Russian, German, Spanish, Hebrew, Tibetan, Arabic, Hindi, French, Swahili, Italian, Chinese, Japanese, and Navajo.

The Sources

Marcus Aurelius (121–180), Roman emperor, stoic philosopher, 25

Markham, Edwin (1882–1940), poet, 22

Milne, A. A. (1882–1956), British author of *Winnie-the-Pooh* and children's poetry, 29

Mohammed (c.570–633), prophet and founder of Islam, 12, 13

Mother Theresa (1910–1997), Founder Missionaries of Charity in India, Nobel Peace Prize Laureate, 7, 17

Paul of Tarsus, Apostle of Jesus, author of New Testament letters, 1, 21

Peace Pilgrim (1908–1981), walking peace advocate, 32

Plato (427–347 BC), Greek philosopher and author, 15

Polese, Richard, 41

Prather, Hugh (b.1938), author, spiritual leader, 11, 19

Ray, Randolph (d.1965), rector of The Little Church Around the Corner in New York City, 6

Reddy, Helen (b.1941), Australian-American pop singer, 28

Renard, Gary, author, 12

Roosevelt, Franklin D. (1882–1945), 32nd President of the United States, 28

Rosten, Leo C. (1908–1997), teacher, author, humorist, 28

Rousseau, Jean Jacques (1712–1778), French social and political philosopher, 3

Sanders, Scott Russell, novelist, essayist, children's writer, 39

Schutte, Meg, 7

Scott, Ralph, 3

Schweitzer, Albert (1875–1965), doctor, writer, organist, theologian, Nobel Peace Prize Laureate, 10

Seneca Lucius Anneaus, Roman statesman, Stoic philosopher, dramatist, 17

Shakespeare, William (1564–1616), English actor, playwright, 29

Simon, Michel (1895–1975), French film actor, 27

Singer, Issac Bashevis (1902–1991), author, Nobel Laureate in Literature, 8

Sivinanda (1887–1963), spiritual teacher, founder the Divine Life Society, 31

Smeltzer, Ruth (via Internet), 22

Sophocles (495–406 BC), Greek playwright, 6, 32

Swedenborg, Emanuel (1688–1772), Swedish scientist, philosopher, mystic, 1

Syrop, Jack (via Internet), 25

The Talmud (c.200–500 AD), Rabbinical commentary on Jewish law, ethics and history; the Babylonian Talmud is considered more comprehensive, 3, 6, 12

Tolstoy, Leo (1828–1910), Russian novelist, 9

Toynbee, Arnold (1889–1975), British historian of world civilizations, 14

Vauvenargues, Luc de Clapiers (1715–1747), French moralist, essayist, 6

Von Suttner, Bertha (1843–1914), author, Nobel Peace Prize Laureate, 22

Wapnick, Kenneth, psychologist, writer, teacher of *A Course in Miracles*, 4, 35

Ward, William Arthur (1921–1994), American author, 5

Webb, Mary (1881–1927), English romantic novelist and poet, 22

Weil, Simone (1909–1943), French writer, teacher, activist, 16

Whitman, Walt (1819–1892), poet, journalist, editor, 33

Wilde, Oscar (1854–1900), Irish playwright, novelist, poet, 19

Wordsworth, William (1770–1850), English poet, 37

Zoroaster (c.1200 BC), Persian founder of Zoroastrianism, practiced today by the Parsi community in India, 16

Kindred Resources

Armstrong, Karen. *The Great Transformation: The Beginning of Our Religious Traditions.* New York: Knopf/Random House, 2006.

Barasch, Marc Ian. *Field Notes on the Compassionate Life.* Emmaus, PA: Rodale Press, 2005.

Brach, Tara. *Radical Acceptance: Embracing Your Life with the Heart of the Buddha.* New York: Bantam/Dell, 2003.

Conover, Sarah, and Valerie Wahl. *Kindness: A Treasury of Buddhist Wisdom for Children and Parents.* Spokane, WA: Eastern Washington University Press, 2001.

Cook, Mary Lou, and Marilyn Gatlin. *Let Your Clown Out of the Closet.* Santa Fe: The Printery, 1992.

de Mallac, Guy. *Gandi's Seven Steps to Global Change.* Santa Fe: Ocean Tree Books, 1989.

Dossey, Larry. *The Extraordinary Healing Power of Ordinary Things: Fourteen Natural Steps to Health and Happiness.* New York: Harmony/Random House, 2006.

Ferrucci, Piero. *The Power of Kindness: The Unexpected Benefits of Leading a Compassionate Life.* New York: Tarcher/Penguin, 2006.

Forrest, Margot Silk. *A Short Course in Kindness: A Little Book on the Relative Importance of Love and the Relative Unimportance of Everything Else.* Cayucos, CA: L. M. Press, 2004.

Gatlin, Marilyn, and Mary Lou Cook. *When I Listen.* Santa Fe: Ocean Tree Books, 1998.

Hawkins, David R. *Power Versus Force: The Hidden Determinants of Human Behavior.* Sedona, AZ: Veritas Publishing, 1998.

Hyde, Catherine Ryan. *Pay It Forward.* New York: Simon and Schuster, 1999.

Jampolsky, Gerald G. *Love Is Letting Go of Fear.* Berkeley, CA: Celestial Arts, 1979.

Kids' Random Acts of Kindness. (foreword by Rosalynn Carter, introduction by Dawna Markova). Berkeley: Conari Press, 1994.

Lozoff, Bo. *It's a Meaningful Life: It Just Takes Practice.* New York: Penguin/Putnam, 2000.

Maathai,Wangari. *Unbound: A Memoir.* New York: Knopf, 2006

McCarty, Meladee, and Hannock McCarty. *Acts of Kindness: How to Make a Gentle Difference.* Dearfield Beach, FL: Health Communications, Inc., 1994.

McCarthy, Coleman. *I'd Rather Teach Peace.* Maryknoll, NY: Orbis, 2002.

McCarthy, Coleman. *A Year of Kindness: 365 Ways to Spread Sunshine.* Dearfield Beach, FL: Health Communications, Inc.,1994.

Paley, Vivian Gussin. *You Can't Say You Can't Play.* Cambridge, MA: Harvard University Press, 1992.

Paley, Vivian Gussin. *The Kindness of Children.* Cambridge, MA: Harvard University Press, 1999.

Peace Pilgrim: Her Life and Works in Her Own Words. Compiled by Some of Her Friends. Santa Fe: Ocean Tree Books, 1982.

Peace Pilgrim. *Steps Toward Inner Peace: Harmonious Principles for Human Living.* Santa Fe: Ocean Tree Books, 1993

Prather, Hugh. *Morning Notes: 365 Meditations to Wake You Up.* Boston: Conari Press, 2006.

Random Acts of Kindness. (introduction by Dawna Markova, foreword by Daphne Rose Kingma). San Francisco: Conari Press, 2002.

Random Acts of Kindness Foundation. *Christian Acts of Kindness.* Berkeley: A Grace House Publication, Conari Press, 1999.

Salzberg, Susan. *Loving Kindness: The Revolutionary Art of Happiness.* Boston: Shambala Publications, Inc.,1995.

Sanders, Scott Russell. *A Private History of Awe.* New York: Farrar, Straus and Giroux, 2006.

Victories without Violence. Compiled by A. Ruth Fry. Santa Fe: Ocean Tree Books, 1986.

Wapnick, Kenneth. *The Healing Power of Kindness: Vol. I: Releasing Judgement, Vol. II: Forgiving Our Limitations.* Temecula, CA: Foundation for A Course in Miracles, 2004, 2005.

About the Compilers

Mary Lou Cook lives in Santa Fe and is a calligrapher, teacher, mother of three, and author or co-author of twelve books. She is co-founder of the New Mexico Department of Peace, an ordained bishop in The Eternal Life Church, a chaplain of the New Mexico State Legislature, official calligrapher for the City of Santa Fe, and a busy wedding officiant. She has been named a Santa Fe Living Treasure. She is a member of the International Women's Forum, founder of the MLC Creativity Center, and led a *Course in Miracles* group for over two decades. She was a staff member for the Peace Corps and served as president of the Children's Arts Program of the Milwaukee Arts Center.

Jan Lurie also lives in Santa Fe and has been a theater costumer, taught costuming, worked in early television production, was a member of the Delaware State Arts Council and Community Arts Coordinator for the State of Delaware. She has been a mental health counselor and workshop leader; started the first *Course in Miracles* group in Delaware and was also ordained in the Eternal Life Church along the way. She is a wife and the mother of two children.

Richard Polese has been a journalist, writer, Santa Fe weekly newspaper and magazine editor, a surgical technician, bartender, hands-on adobe house builder, and a book publisher since 1983. He wrote *Discovering Dixie* and co-authored *Passions in Print, Private Press Artistry in New Mexico* and *The New Deal: A 75th Anniversary Celebration*. He was one of the compilers of *Peace Pilgrim: Her Life and Work in Her Own Words*. He is ordained in The Eternal Life Church, father of three children, executive director of the New Mexico Book Association, and serves on the Santa Fe Board of Education.

You may order copies of
The Book of Kindness
for friends and family directly from
the publisher if it is not available
at your bookstore.
Write your check or money order for $12.50,
plus $3.50 for packaging, and mail to:
Ocean Tree Books
Post Office Box 1295
Santa Fe, New Mexico 87504

Discover other useful and inspiring books
at www.oceantree.com.
We are pleased to mail copies of
The Book of Kindness to any
address you request.